Happy Birthday, Kit—
With much affection
and admiration
"from Alabama Relatives"

January 20, 1991

ALABAMA MEMORIES

COVER/TITLE PAGE. WHITWOOD HOME, TALLADEGA

ALABAMA MEMORIES

PHOTOGRAPHS
BY CHIP COOPER

PREFACE BY JACK W. WARNER
ESSAY BY MARIDITH WALKER
DESIGNED BY GARY CREEK

GALLERY BOOKS
An Imprint of W.H. Smith Publishers, Inc.
112 Madison Avenue
New York , New York 10016

This edition first published 1989 in New York by Gallery Books, an
imprint of W.H. Smith Publishers, Inc. 112 Madison Avenue, New
York 10016

ISBN O-8317-0200-1

Gallery Books are available for bulk purchase for sales promotions
and premium use. For details write or telephone the Manager of
Special Sales, W.H. Smith Publishers, Inc., 112 Madison Avenue, New
York, New York 10016. (212) 536-6600.

D·E·D·I·C·A·T·I·O·N

For my children, Eliza and Brandon, whose love and understanding
made this book possible.

8. BOTTOM LAND FOREST, STATE ROAD 3, BALDWIN COUNTY

P·R·E·F·A·C·E
Jack W. Warner

Our company is over 105 years old, and one of the very first to pioneer papermaking from southern pine (1912). We arrived in Alabama in 1927 and have lived happily ever after. It was a great state then and a greater state today. I know of no place in the country that has more space to move around or a brighter future than Alabama. It is truly "the great surprise."

In those early days of author Carl Carmer's *Stars Fell on Alabama* our way of life was so gentle, so relaxing, so wonderfully steeped in old traditions that we wanted simply to keep it that way. Every day was Christmas Eve.

Hudson Strode's writing classes produced such books as *Rachel's Children, From Hell to Breakfast, Lanterns on the Levee.* It was the Old South with Christmas in the canebrake, hunting on those cold misty mornings, upriver excursions and barbecue chicken on the old riverboat "E-Z Kraft." A way of life nobody wanted to turn in for the hustle and bustle of urban blight. In fact I guess our attitude was that it all was too good for them. Let's just keep it for ourselves.

But when Harper Lee published her Pulitzer Prize novel *To Kill a Mockingbird* in 1960, concerning life in a small Alabama town in the 1930s, we came to accept "Miss Lee's conviction that we must recognize and accept our place in national and international life, and accept the consequences for doing so."* So we are moving ahead and out of our old ways. Yet we have kept the good of our heritage, and, at the same time, we are creating jobs and living standards for our people.

There *is* a new stirring in Alabama. We are on the move. The visual arts, music, drama, and sports are all mixed in with a gentler, more relaxed way of life. We truly have much to offer in our varied and dynamic culture.

*Fred Erisman, "The Romantic Regionalism of Harper Lee," *Alabama Review,* XXVI.

10. REFLECTIONS IN OLD DOORS, WHATLEY HOME, TUSKEGEE

E·S·S·A·Y

Maridith Walker

Surely nobody else would think to stop here: a house that barely earns that name, its porch sagging, its windows boarded, an old car forlorn in the front yard. Surely this is an embarrassment, a place one would pass with averted eyes, loathe to acknowledge that this is part of our southern landscape.

Chip Cooper, on this unusually balmy January afternoon, insists on stopping. He's stopped here more than once, and he keeps coming back, full of the discoveries the place yields.

He hardly glances at the house. What draws him is a tangle of woody stems scarcely more than sticks. Splayed like skinny fingers, they rise from a bed of clover that provides one of the few touches of color in the otherwise drab yard.

Focused on that setting, the camera is able to filter, to select, to sort through a jumble of impressions the eye takes in and to pull from those one unexpectedly beautiful scene. The result is a photograph (page 140) that creates the illusion of an enormous forest. What has seemed to the quick glance a common, even tawdry, scene has suddenly become a landscape dramatically larger than life. Cooper has evoked an image very few people could imagine from the setting.

That patient search through the everyday landscape of Alabama life is the hallmark of Chip Cooper's work. Look through the images in this book, and you'll see that nothing is too ordinary to escape the potential for transformation—not merely a beautiful photograph, but an image that lingers, generating a strong sense of place: the fading side of a warehouse (page 144B); the turret of a Victorian home lit by the late afternoon sun (page 86B); an old wagon, abandoned and mottled from years of exposure (page 40A); a young pine seedling green as spring on a rainy winter day (page 169). Our fields, our farms, our homes, our small towns . . . the artifacts that stand as mute testimony to a passing way of life. These are, for Chip Cooper, the essence of Alabama.

E·S·S·A·Y

From the tangle of sensations that surround us, he extracts details that can speak to us in their simplicity. The scene may be representational, an easily recognized landmark in the life we know. Or it may be a photographic abstract, one feature of a larger view that the camera reinterprets and gives back as a design we would have missed. In such a photo, the fading tin of a neglected outbuilding becomes an interlocking grid (page 102) whose beauty resides not in the whole but in the part. By forcing us to focus attention on the small as well as the large, Cooper offers us unexpected delights buried in the all-too-ordinary complexities of our lives.

More than anything, his work is driven by the pressures of time. In part, he senses we are losing once proud structures and landscapes that are now falling prey to time's relentless erosion. But more important, he senses that we ourselves are losing the time and space to look around and to absorb the beauty the state has to give. In this juncture of changing times, he feels compelled to preserve those rapidly departing scenes.

The Alabama Cooper photographs derives from a slower, more agrarian life, an age when people sat on front porches, worked side by side in the fields, stopped for conversations with one another, and took the time to know their environment.

Those days are, increasingly, past. An era that offers the welcome prosperity of new industry and new technology brings with it a more urgent lifestyle and different priorities. We preserve the obvious artifacts as testimony to a grand past, but we fail to see the common ones, allowing physical structures—old barns, old homes, old stores, old churches—as well as nature's structures—groves of trees, pastures, streams—to fall into disuse and disarray. Those common signs of a commonly held past—unpretentious as the land itself—find their way into image after image Cooper shoots.

For him, Alabama's interstate highways have become emblematic of the New South, both its sense of time and its way of viewing itself. On the superhighway system, Cooper believes, we travel an anonymous landscape. What we see as we speed across

E·S·S·A·Y

our state, if we bother to look at all, is a countryside of uniformity: twin ribbons of asphalt that work efficiently but show us little. As an artist, Cooper bemoans the fact that our small towns, long the center of a unique culture, have for many of us become no more than exit signs whose names we may remember but whose personalities we rarely know. Mooresville. Newbern. Magnolia Springs. Mentone. Cherokee. Waverly.

In this book, he returns to those places, capturing them with a grace that makes them timeless. His visits are not sentimental, not merely a desire to return to a romanticized past, because he firmly believes in the progress Alabama has committed itself to. Rather, he seeks out those small towns and back highways to look deeper into a way of life that makes Alabama distinct. His visits and the photos he returns with are a way of affirming identity, preserving the beauty of Alabama and the legacy of memories that bond the old with the new.

It is not surprising that an artist so concerned with time should spend so much of it in search of his particular visions. Cooper has traveled the state ten times over, looking, absorbing, selecting sites that appeal to him. At times, he returns to them with the light in mind, content to wait for just that angle and just that moment when the scene becomes more than a pretty landscape. At times, he must catch the shot as he finds it, working spontaneously in the split second he discovers all elements blending together. "This is why I love photography," Cooper states. "It gives me the option of waiting for that decisive moment or reacting immediately to what I see."

As photography has become more technical and more complex, Cooper has also felt the need to simplify his creative process. His work, often compared to paintings, shows deeply felt resonances, but they are suggested by the greatest simplicity: the spare lines of a white picket fence before a frame church (page 47A); the eloquent isolation of a single tombstone (page 59). In mood and technique, Cooper's photographs reflect the strong influence of a group of southern painters whose work he admires, among them Richard Zoellner, Beau Redmond, and Evan Wilson.

E·S·S·A·Y

Despite the differences in medium, he has learned from these artists the value of selectivity. Recognizing that they have the freedom to alter the reality they represent, Cooper has adapted that way of seeing into his own work. He approaches his subjects much as these southern artists do, focusing on what he calls the essentials of the scene. To him that means eliminating extraneous details and using the elements of nature, particularly light, to convey what he sees as the heart of his subject.

"My greatest desire," he has said, "is to suggest to a viewer some of the emotion I experience when I photograph a particular scene. I saw an old warehouse in Cherokee (page 114) in broad daylight and could see its potential. Seen in that light it was scarcely more than a delapidated building. So I waited until twilight, framing it in a band of darkness that was broken only by a small porch light. The result was a structure that looked entirely different, an image that suggested the original dignity of the building."

When you travel the backroads of Alabama with Chip Cooper, it is next to impossible not to feel a sense of the extraordinary in our ordinary surroundings. On a drizzly, miserable January day, he suddenly stops his car on a bridge crossing the Tennessee River. Behind him, cars and trucks thunder past, the bridge shuddering and groaning with each swish of tires. He's oblivious to the noise or to the curiosity of passersby. As a flock of ducks take to the sky, he trains his camera on a scene far below, where a quiet backwater belies the clamor of traffic above. Here, as light begins to fade into darkness, he captures the stillness and beauty of a low fog hanging just over the water.

Turning to go, he pauses. "I photograph what many people see every day but don't take the time to stop and think about," he says. "I hope that my photographs will encourage people to slow down and look again." In this book of photographs that span the width and length of Alabama, Chip Cooper has assured that we will not only look, but that we will return again and again to the scenes that we share in memory.

PLATES

16. FROST ON HARDWOODS, COUNTY ROAD 49, COLBERT COUNTY

17. FLAG WITH PICKET FENCE, TALLADEGA

18. CHIMNEYS, COUNTY ROAD 290, CHAMBERS COUNTY

19. RED WAREHOUSE WALL, U.S. ROAD 82, BARBOUR COUNTY

20. GRAIN BIN, COUNTY ROAD 56, MARION COUNTY

21. WHITE FENCE AND COLONIAL HOME, CHEROKEE

22A. SUNRISE, COUNTY ROAD 63, MARENGO COUNTY
22B. SUNSET. CHEAHA STATE PARK, CLAY COUNTY

23. INTERIOR, WHATLEY HOME, TUSKEGEE

24. ANGELS IN CEMETERY, MOBILE

25. CHAMBERS COUNTY COURTHOUSE, LAFAYETTE

26. ENGLISH IVY COVERING WAREHOUSE WALL, CASTLEBERRY

27. RED ROOF REFLECTED IN WINDOW, NEWBERN

28. SHUTTERS, NEWBERN

29A. STORE FRONTS, DEMOPOLIS
29B. WAREHOUSE FRONT, COUNTY ROAD 6, CONECUH COUNTY

30-31. ROYAL CROWN COLA SIGN, STATE ROAD 171, TUSCALOOSA COUNTY

32. DIRT ROAD, STATE ROAD 17, LAMAR COUNTY

33A. DETAIL OF GREEN BARN, VALLEY HEAD
33B. GREEN BARN, VALLEY HEAD

34. FIELD OF BUTTERCUPS, STATE ROAD 25, WILCOX COUNTY

35. RAY'S FURNITURE STORE WALL, CALERA

36. ARCHED DOOR ON RED WALL, DEMOPOLIS

37. PRINCESS TREE IN WINDOW, LINDEN

38. VIRGINIA PINE AND SOIL STRATA, PHENIX CITY

39. SUNRISE OVER GULF OF MEXICO, GULF SHORES

40A. CLOWN WAGON, COUNTY ROAD 7, LOWNDES COUNTY
40B. DETAIL OF CLOWN WAGON, COUNTY ROAD 7, LOWNDES COUNTY

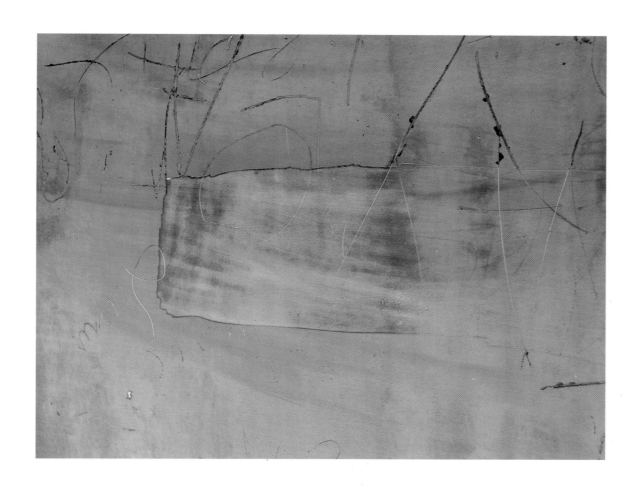

41. DETAIL OF CLOWN WAGON, COUNTY ROAD 7, LOWNDES COUNTY

42. BROOM SEDGE IN WINTER, COUNTY ROAD 77, ETOWAH COUNTY

43. MOCK ORANGE TREE AND GREEN BARN, NEWBERN

44. CAFE, STATE ROAD 117, DEKALB COUNTY

45. FOUR WINDOWS, EUTAW

46A. YELLOW STRIPES AND FALL FOLIAGE, DESOTO STATE PARK, DEKALB COUNTY
46B. RED MAPLE LEAF, TALLADEGA NATIONAL FOREST, CLEBURNE COUNTY

47A. FRONT OF CHURCH, MOORESVILLE
47B. PICKET FENCE, STATE ROAD 14, GREENE COUNTY

48. SIDE OF TRUCK TRAILER, U.S. ROAD 42, BALDWIN COUNTY

49. SIDE OF TRUCK TRAILER, U.S. ROAD 42, BALDWIN COUNTY

50. CROSSING RAILWAY TRACKS, VALLEY HEAD

51A. SHADOWS AND RED DOOR, MOORESVILLE
51B. FALL LIGHT ON MOORESVILLE POST OFFICE, MOORESVILLE

52. OUT BUILDINGS, BEATRICE

53. ST. ANDREWS EPISCOPAL CHURCH AND IRON FENCE, PRAIRIEVILLE

54. SUNSET, PINE BEACH

55. ARCHED DOOR AT TWILIGHT, TALLADEGA

56. RIVER BIRCHES, TENNESSEE RIVER BACKWATER, MADISON COUNTY

57. INDIAN MOUNDS AT DUSK, MOUND STATE PARK, MOUNDVILLE

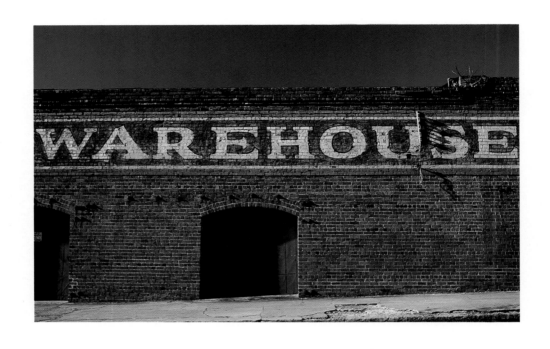

58A. SIDE OF WAREHOUSE, ROANOKE
58B. BLACK FENCE AND PASTURE, STATE ROAD 59, BALDWIN COUNTY

59. CEMETERY DRIVE AND FLAG, LAFAYETTE

60. DESERTED BUILDING REFLECTED IN GREEN WINDOW, DEMOPOLIS

61. GOSPORT CASH STORE, U.S. HIGHWAY 84, CLARKE COUNTY

62. BLUE LAGOON, ROMAR BEACH

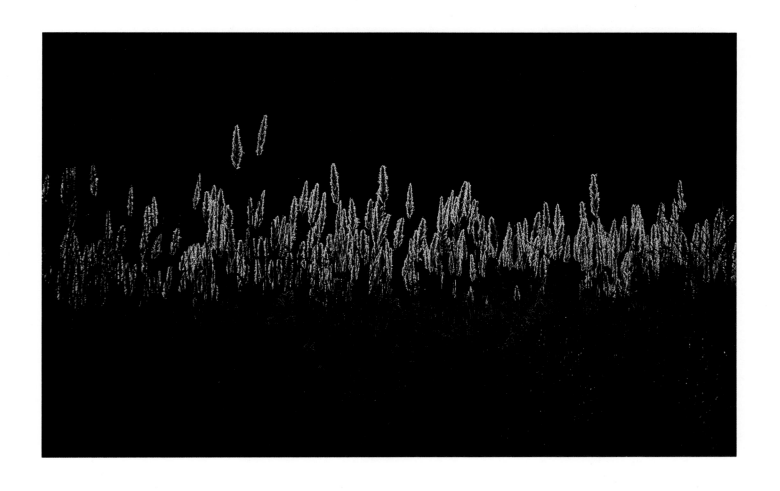

63. GRASS PLUMES, JASPER

64-65. REFLECTED FALL FOLIAGE, LITTLE RIVER, DEKALB COUNTY

66. TWO WINDOWS AT SUNSET, EUTAW

67. RIP-RAP AND TREES ON RIVER BANK, GREENE COUNTY

68. RUINS AT FORKS OF CYPRESS, LAUDERDALE COUNTY

69. LATTICE ON DESERTED HOME, OPELIKA

70. RED LUMBER, CHEROKEE

71A. RED WAREHOUSE, EUFAULA
71B. NO SMOKING PLEASE AND WAREHOUSE WALL, EUFAULA

72. CYPRESS SWAMP, COOK'S BEND HUNTING CLUB, GREENE COUNTY

73. DUSK OVER PASTURE, PAULLING PLACE, COUNTY ROAD 63, MARENGO COUNTY

74A. MARSH GRASS, COUNTY ROAD 161, COTTON BAYOU, ORANGE BEACH
74B. TAIL-END OF TRAILER, FOLEY

75. RED BARN IN AUTUMN, COUNTY ROAD 89, DEKALB COUNTY

76. PINK DOGWOOD BLOOMS, MONTGOMERY

77. COKE BOTTLES ON GROCERY WALL, EUTAW

78A. RED TRAILER AND SWEET GUM TREE, STATE ROAD 171, TUSCALOOSA COUNTY
78B. WHEAT FIELD AND WILLOW OAK IN WINTER, STATE ROAD 21, TALLADEGA COUNTY

79A. FALL FOLIAGE, GUNTERSVILLE
79B. LICHEN AND SUGAR MAPLES, DESOTO STATE PARK, DEKALB COUNTY

80. STOP SIGN AND YELLOW BUILDING, VALLEY HEAD

81. PRAIRIE CONE FLOWERS, STATE ROAD 61, PERRY COUNTY

82. VICTORIAN RAILING, OPELIKA

83. KUDZU AND FINLEY'S TRUCK STOP, DIXONS MILL

84. SUNSET REFLECTED IN WINDOW, TUSCALOOSA

85. FRONT OF FARM HOUSE, STATE HIGHWAY 21, TALLADEGA COUNTY

86A. DETAIL OF VICTORIAN PORCH, ROANOKE
86B. VICTORIAN HOME AT DUSK, ROANOKE

87. MAPLE BRANCHES, FORT PAYNE

88. FARM ROAD WITH PECAN TREES, STATE HIGHWAY 13, MARENGO COUNTY

89. IVY AND WINDOW REFLECTIONS, NEWBERN

90. YELLOW STRIPES AND BRIDGE, GAINESVILLE

91. TWILIGHT REFLECTIONS ON SIDE OF WALL, STATE ROAD 7, GREENE COUNTY

92. OLD FIELD IN WINTER, HIGHWAY 79, MACON COUNTY

93. RED MAPLE LEAF, TALLADEGA NATIONAL FOREST, CALHOUN COUNTY

94-95. FENCES, TALLADEGA

96. OLD CHEVY AND BUILDING, STATE ROAD 187, FRANKLIN COUNTY

97. FRONT OF HOUSE WITH RED DOOR, MOORESVILLE

98. HORSE WEED AND YELLOW FLOWERS, COUNTY ROAD 23, CHOCTAW COUNTY

99. THREE ARCHES, EUTAW

100. TULIPS IN SNOW, UNIVERSITY OF ALABAMA, TUSCALOOSA

101. FRONT OF VICTORIAN HOME, U.S. HIGHWAY 431, RANDOLPH COUNTY

102. TIN SIDING, STATE ROAD 69, HALE COUNTY

103A. COLA ON BRICK WALL, DEMOPOLIS
103B. MARSH GRASS WITH STICKS, ROMAR BEACH

104. DOGWOOD IN BLOOM, TUSCALOOSA

105. FROST ON JAPANESE QUINCE, FLORENCE

106. LE HAIR WINDOW, EUTAW

107. FROSTBITTEN CAMELLIAS, EUFAULA

108A. MOSS-COVERED SANDSTONE WITH TREES, DISMALS, FRANKLIN COUNTY
108B. MOSSY ROCKS AND HEMLOCKS, DISMALS, FRANKLIN COUNTY

109. FRONT OF ''THE SPOT,'' MARION

110. DARK SOIL AND GREEN FIELD, INTERSTATE 65, LIMESTONE COUNTY

111A. DOORWAY, TODDLE INN SCHOOL, TALLADEGA
111B. DOGWOOD IN AUTUMN, TUSCALOOSA

112. DAR HOME, MOBILE

113. CYPRESS TREE WITH SPANISH MOSS, U.S. HIGHWAY 43, MOBILE COUNTY

114. FRONT OF WAREHOUSE AT NIGHT, CHEROKEE

115. SUNSET ON BACKWATERS OF TOMBIGBEE RIVER, MARENGO COUNTY

116. AFTERNOON SUN ON HOME, STATE HIGHWAY 1, RANDOLPH COUNTY

117. SIDE OF RED BARN, STATE HIGHWAY 61, HALE COUNTY

118. PECAN ORCHARD, STATE HIGHWAY 42, BALDWIN COUNTY

119. ALSOBROOK MANSION, CUSSETA

120A. RED TIN ROOF, NEWBERN
120B. FALL COLORS, TALLADEGA NATIONAL FOREST, BIBB COUNTY

121. COTTON WAREHOUSE, EUFAULA

122. SIDE OF BUILDINGS, FAUNSDALE

123. ICE ON TREES, FLORENCE

124. FRONT PORCH WITH ROCKERS, OPELIKA

125. OLD ROCKING CHAIR, RANGE

126. SUNSET, ALABAMA POINT, BALDWIN COUNTY

127. GREENLEAF STALKS, STATE HIGHWAY 69, WALKER COUNTY

128. DESOTO FALLS WITH AUTUMN FOLIAGE, DESOTO STATE PARK, DEKALB COUNTY

129A. SIDE OF TRUCK TRAILER, STATE ROAD 42, BALDWIN COUNTY
129B. SALTWATER LAGOON, ROMAR BEACH

130. REFLECTIONS ON LAKE MARTIN, TALLAPOOSA COUNTY

131A. ORANGE GLIDER, WAVERLY
131B. WAREHOUSE WALL, DEMOPOLIS

132A. RED MAPLE LEAVES, MENTONE
132B. SUGAR MAPLE TREES, LITTLE RIVER CANYON, CHEROKEE COUNTY

133. GUILIO NUCCIO CAMELLIA, DEE DAVIS GREENHOUSE, TUSCALOOSA

134. SHADOWS WITH GAZEBO, FORK OF COUNTY ROADS 10 AND 26, MACON COUNTY

135. TULIPS WITH PRESIDENT'S MANSION, UNIVERSITY OF ALABAMA, TUSCALOOSA

136. MOSS AND FERN-COVERED ROCKS, DISMALS, FRANKLIN COUNTY

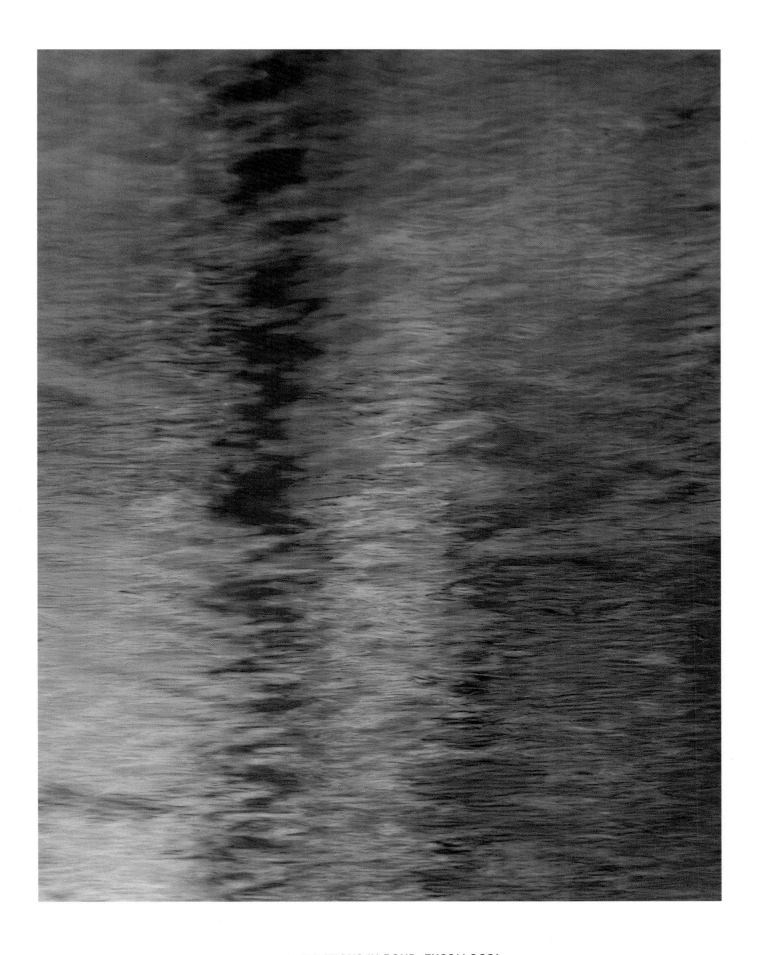

137. REFLECTIONS IN POND, TUSCALOOSA

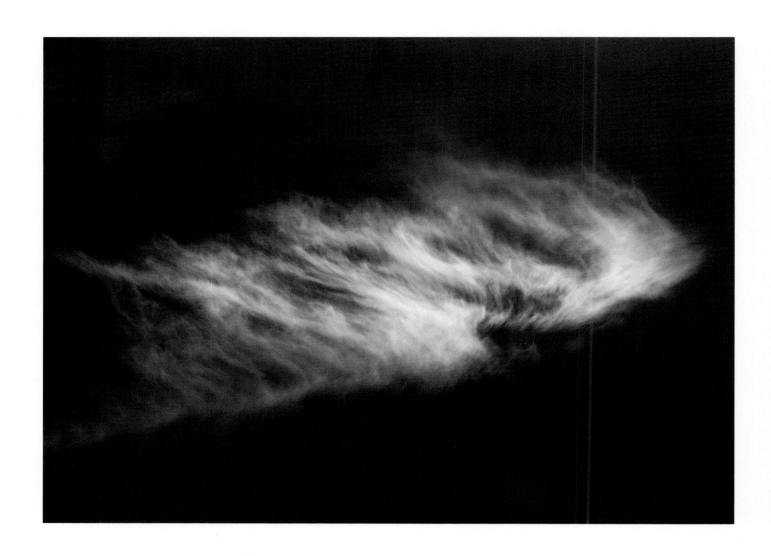

138. EARLY SPRING SUNSET, BIRMINGHAM

139A. CANYON RIDGE, LITTLE RIVER CANYON, CHEROKEE COUNTY
139B. ICE-COVERED MAPLES, FLORENCE

140. CLOVER AND STEMS, STATE ROAD 69, HALE COUNTY

141. PEANUT WAGONS, EUFAULA

142. LIVE OAKS, MAGNOLIA SPRINGS

143. RED CEDAR AND MANSION, VALLEY HEAD

144A. SIDE OF BUILDING WITH ARCHED DOOR, EUTAW
144B. DETAIL OF BUILDING WALL, EUTAW

145. ISLAND IN TENNESSEE RIVER BACKWATERS, LIMESTONE COUNTY

146. REFLECTION OF STOCKTON CITY HALL, STOCKTON

147. LATE AFTERNOON LIGHT ON STOCKTON CITY HALL, STOCKTON

148. TREE IN BLOOM, WHITWOOD HOME, TALLADEGA

149. BUILDING ON WHATLEY FARM, HAVANA JUNCTION

150. TWILIGHT ON POND, PAULLING PLACE, MARENGO COUNTY

151. WINTER SUN, PAULLING PLACE, MARENGO COUNTY

152A. AFTER-RAINSTORM SUNSET, WHEELER REFUGE, DECATUR
152B. BROOM SEDGE WITH HOME, COUNTY ROAD 55, CHAMBERS COUNTY

153. DUSK ON LAKE GUNTERSVILLE, JACKSON COUNTY

154. NIGHT FALL ON WINTER FIELD, HUNTSVILLE

155. LITTLE RIVER, LITTLE RIVER CANYON, CHEROKEE COUNTY

156. OLD CHURCH ON DIRT HILL, STATE HIGHWAY 13, MARENGO COUNTY

157. DETAIL OF OLD CHURCH DOOR, STATE HIGHWAY 13, MARENGO COUNTY

158A. SALTWATER GRASS, GULF SHORES
158B. REFLECTION OF MOVIE THEATRE, EUTAW

159. WISTERIA WITH FALL COLORS, HUNTSVILLE

160-61. PECAN GROVE, FOLEY

162. PASTURE AT DUSK, ALABAMA RIVER, MONROE COUNTY

163. REDBUD, BREWTON

164. SWAIM HOME IRON FENCE, TUSCALOOSA

165. SILO IN FIELD, STATE ROAD 165, RUSSELL COUNTY

166. DOUBLE GREEN DOORS WITH LIGHT, COUNTY ROAD 11, LEE COUNTY

167A. SMUT EYE GROCERY STORE, SMUT EYE
167B. DETAIL OF SMUT EYE GROCERY STORE, SMUT EYE

168. HEMLOCKS IN HARDWOOD FOREST, DISMALS, FRANKLIN COUNTY

169. LOBLOLLY SEEDLING, MORGAN COUNTY

170. SUNSET ON WEBB HOME, DEMOPOLIS

171. LAUNDRY ON LINE, COUNTY ROAD 21, GREENE COUNTY

172. MOTTLED MAPLE LEAVES, STATE HIGHWAY 7, JEFFERSON COUNTY

173A. OLD JAIL, FAUNSDALE
173B. SUNSET, STATE ROAD 53, MONTGOMERY COUNTY

174. FAT MAN'S SQUEEZE, DISMALS, FRANKLIN COUNTY

175. WINTER WHEAT FIELD, COUNTY ROAD 207, TALLADEGA COUNTY

176. REFLECTIONS IN THREE WINDOWS, NEWBERN

177. LOOKING OUT OF WINDOW, EUTAW

178. OLD POST OFFICE, DIXONS MILL

179. DETAIL OF OLD POST OFFICE, DIXONS MILL

180. HOLLY BERRIES, U.S. HIGHWAY 80, DALLAS COUNTY

181. DUSK IN THE MOUNTAINS, MENTONE

182. CORN SHUCKS HAY, COUNTY ROAD 6, WALKER COUNTY

183. FRONT OF OLD HOME, STATE ROAD 263, BUTLER COUNTY

184A. WEED FIELD WITH CIRRUS CLOUDS, COUNTY ROAD 44, MARENGO COUNTY
184B. WINDOW ON PINK HOUSE, TALLADEGA

185. EVENING MIST, ALABAMA RIVER, MONROE COUNTY

186. EVENING LIGHT ON RED WAREHOUSE, EUFAULA

187. SUNSET ON POND, STATE ROAD 13, MARENGO COUNTY

188. BLUE ROOF WITH RED CHIMNEY, MONTROSE

189. LEE COUNTY COURTHOUSE, OPELIKA

190. BAYSIDE MARSH, ROMAR BEACH
BACK COVER. FARM ROAD WITH PECAN TREES, STATE HIGHWAY 13, MARENGO COUNTY

A·C·K·N·O·W·L·E·D·G·E·M·E·N·T·S

This body of work would never have been possible without the dedication and constant encouragement of Doris Hurst Leapard, Bob Monfore, Gary Creek, Maridith Walker, Sandra Still, and Caroline Davis.

I am also extremely grateful for the support and understanding of Joe Pierce, Jack Leigh, Dr. Phil Norris, George and Suzanne Wolfe, Dr. Doug Jones, Dr. Joab Thomas, Dr. Jerry Oldshue, Mike Ellis, Bob Wells, The University of Alabama Natural History Museum, Dick Zoellner, David Adnett, Mary Jolley, Bill Wagnon, Belinda Lane and the Pleasure Island Chamber of Commerce, Sam Bartle, University Relations Photographic Department with Rickey Yanaura, Alice Wilson, Diana Moore, and Janice Pope, Bill Bassett and John's Photo for the contribution of film, and Lanny Crawford and Photographics, Inc. for help with typography.

A·L·A·B·A·M·A M·E·M·O·R·I·E·S

Was conceived and edited by Sandra Still. It was designed by Gary Creek with print production by Mary Boettger. The type was set in Novarese by Pauline Hutson of Photographics, Inc., Tuscaloosa, Alabama. Print production was by Kingsley Associates, Wilton, Connecticut.

Limited edition prints are available of *Alabama Memories* photographs.